What Honeybees Do

by Virginia Wright

Buzzzzzzz₀₀₀₀

What Honeybees Do

Written by Virginia Wright
Nature Photos and Art by Virginia Wright

For "Free" Preschool – Kindergarten Themed Activity Pages Visit
Author Web: http://www.virginiawright.com
Email: info@virginiawright.com
For bulk ordering, & information, address: Book Fulfillment
P.O. Box 175
East Machias, Maine 04630

First Edition 2010
Published in the United States of America by
Book-A-Day™

International Standard Book Number: 1451552688
Library of Congress Control Number: 2010904070

Have you read other Virginia Wright Books yet?

- ➢ THE PRINCESS AND THE CASTLE -
  ISBN - 145051054X
- ➢ THE PRINCE AND THE DRAGON -
  ISBN 1451507682
- ➢ CRYING BEAR –
  ISBN 1450587941
- ➢ THE CHRISTMAS SECRET -
  ISBN 1451534280

THIS BOOK BELONGS TO:

_____

Given By: _____

Date Given: _____

Special Note:

Virginia Wright

Dedication

To Abigail (Grammy's Girl) you know
what the buzz is all about...

Acknowledgements

Dave, the natural beekeeper, for if it were not
for you this book wouldn't be possible.

Bob Gillespie thanks for the introduction into
the wonderful world of honeybees.

To my daughter in law Bethany, thanks for all
the help making the wrongs-- right.

Plant flowers that honeybees like.

Foreword

Exploring the Fascinating World of Honeybees...

Surviving and evolving over millions of years; honeybees are one of our most amazing creatures. They provide the essential service of pollinating so many flowers; flowers of trees, shrubs, and plants of many types. In fact, bees and plants have evolved synergistically (like team members) to accommodate the needs of one another. The plants evolved methods to attract the bees to do the job of pollination; while the bees were developing ways to find, carry, store, and best use the bounty of pollen and nectar provided in exchange for their services.

Do all honeybees sting? What do they do with pollen? How do they make honey? Are bees in trouble? What can we do at home to benefit the bees? You will find these answers and more in this book.

Dave Wright, ANAP Beekeeping
http://www.davesbees.com

Buzzzzzzzz What Honeybees Do

Honeybees *are* amazing creatures, for they are insects that provide us with golden sweet food known as honey.

Let's start with what honey looks and tastes like, as both can vary between each collection. The color of honey can be pale yellow, golden, or dark amber as you can see in the photo below.

The taste varies too. The lighter color honey usually has a milder tasting flavor, while the darker color honey can have a stronger, distinctive taste. It just depends on the plant source (flowers) the honeybees have gathered the nectar from.

The honeybee's home is called a hive. You can find a colony of honeybees naturally out in the wild in a hollow tree. But outside of nature, there are a few other types of hives. In some countries, beekeepers still use Skep's which are made from natural materials such as straw, as shown in the photo below.

Some natural beekeepers use the Kenya Top Bar Hive (KTBH) due to their simplicity. The Langstroth Hive (Lang) is traditionally used more often by commercial beekeepers that keep bees to sell the bees' honey.

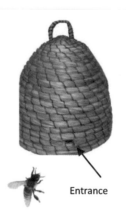

Entrance

A Skep, as shown in the photo to the right is a type of beehive.

++++++++++++

In the United States, Skep's are not allowed to be used for beekeeping. They are generally used for decoration.

BEE SKEP

This type of beehive is made of straw and coiled around in a circle with a single entrance into the hive.

Kenya Top Bar Hive (Has no frame, only top bar)

Langstroth Hive (Has enclosed frame, top, bottom and sides)

In the hive, there is a mother bee--called the *Queen*. She is larger than all the other honeybees, especially in length. In addition to the queen bee, there are worker bees and drones in the hive with varying jobs.

Hexagonal (six-sided) wax cells are made by the bees. This is where the honey is stored. Below is a photo of a queen bee and workers on newly made honeycomb.

Queen

Look at the very long body of the queen and the perfectly shaped wax cells the workers have made.

In the beginning, the queen is chosen larvae (a worm-like insect) and raised by workers. She is fed *Royal Jelly* which is a healthy food source with the nutrition that is needed for making her turn into a big, strong bee. The queen is fed this super nutritious food all of the time which is what contributes to her larger size; where the other bees only get a little bit when they are maturing (growing up).

The bees have many different jobs inside and outside of the hive. Worker bees care for the queen, gather pollen and nectar, and clean the hive. They are also able to regulate the temperature in the hive. In the summer they cool the hive by rapidly fanning their wings. When winter comes they stay warm by grouping together and vibrating their wing muscles.

Nurse bees, which are also considered workers, feed and raise the developing bees, called *brood.* You will also find some workers that are called guard bees, guarding the entrance of the hive from wasps, ants, and other interfering insects.

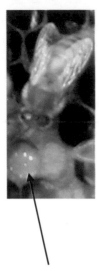

Capped Brood

(Developing Honeybees)

+++++++

➢ From an egg to an adult bee--workers take about 21 days.

➢ Drones take about 24 days.

➢ Queens take only about 16 days.

Bee Larvae   Capped Honey

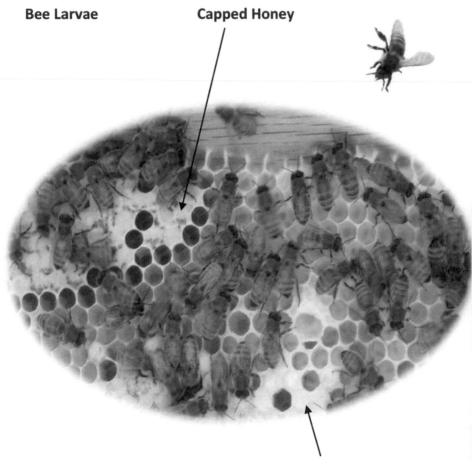

Capped Brood

In a beehive, there are a few hundred boy bees-- called, *drones.* And there can be as many as 40,000+ girl bees-- called, *workers.*

As mentioned earlier, each bee has a job to do in the hive, born with this instinct so as to carry out their duties. The queen bee's job is laying eggs; she almost always stays in the beehive and lets the workers tend to her needs.

+++++++

DRONE BEE (Pictured on tip of the finger)

Drones don't sting, as they have no stinger; they are larger than workers, but not as large as a queen.

Worker bees hunt for nectar and pollen. Nectar is a sweet liquid that the bees get from the flower. Pollen is the yellow powdery stuff that bees get from flowers and also that you see around the bee's legs in the photo below. The pollen is carried back to the hive on the honeybee's legs with their pollen baskets or sometimes called pollen buckets which are on either side of their bodies.

(Fine hairs shown here on the honeybee)

Pollen (Pollen is full of protein and is food for bees)

Actually, what is referred to as being pollen baskets, is just a patch of hairs that the bees pack the pollen into so they can carry it back to the hive. Once at the hive, they place the pollen in little chambers of wax, which they have built for storing pollen, nectar, and laying eggs in.

Compound eye, one of five eyes - The honeybee has two compound eyes and three small ocelli (simple eye with one lens) in between the compound eyes.

Tongue

Flower: Coltsfoot a honeybee favorite

It is not unusual for a honeybee to fly two miles and in extreme cases up to six miles away from the beehive to hunt for food.

Once the bees have gathered their nectar, they carry it back to the hive in one of their two stomachs called the *honey stomach*. Next, they carefully place it into the cells of the comb. To make it into honey, they fan the nectar with their wings to evaporate or draw off the extra water in it. When the right amount of water is out, they put just enough wax on the top to seal the honey in the honeycomb. The honey is stored for the girl bees to live on during the winter months when there aren't many nectar sources. The boy bees are kicked out of the hive before winter so that the workers don't have to feed them.

Look at the wings; they are tattered from all the flights...

Flower: Honeybee on Ohio Goldenrod

Winter Bee Yard (Apiary)

In the winter bees stay warm inside the hive by clustering together.

Langstroth Hive

Kenya Top Bar Hive;
after the snow melts.

Some hobbyist beekeepers will not take any honey off the hive if honey stores are low. This is to ensure that the bees have enough honey stored to live on over the winter.

When commercial beekeepers keep bees for a living and take off honey from the hive, they will feed the honeybees sugar water through the winter to prevent them from starving.

(If you find a swarm of bees don't use bug spray, call a local beekeeper)

The honeybee-- our greatest pollinator

Honeybee Body Parts

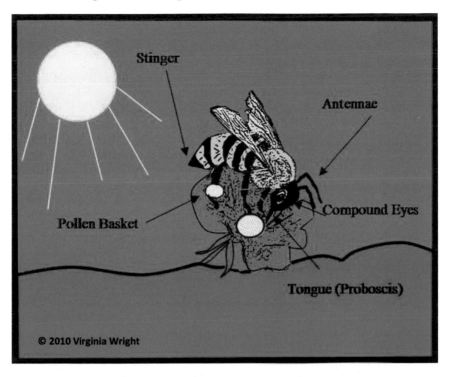

Stinger

Antennae

Compound Eyes

Pollen Basket

Tongue (Proboscis)

© 2010 Virginia Wright

Now you know what the buzzzzzzzz is all about, and have learned the basics of what honeybees do.

Kenya Top Bar Hive

Beekeeper

Butterfly weed

Some plants that bee's buzz over

Sumac

Honeybee in flight... instinctively going for the flowers she knows has the best nectar sources.

From flower to flower, the honeybee takes flight, buzz, buzz, buzzzzzzzz.

Aster

Blackberry Blossoms

Queen Anne's Lace

Snowdrop

Thistle

More plants that honeybees like

- ➤ Alsike Clover
- ➤ Crimson Clover
- ➤ White & Yellow Sweet Clovers
- ➤ Buckwheat
- ➤ Milkweed
- ➤ Goldenrod
- ➤ Pumpkin, Squash, Cucumber and Herbs, e.g., Oregano
- ➤ Lemon Balm
- ➤ Sedum Autumn Joy
- ➤ Dandelion
- ➤ Purple Loosestrife
- ➤ Butterfly Weed
- ➤ Bee Balm
- ➤ Heather
- ➤ Coneflower
- ➤ Wingstem

Coneflower

Trees that honeybees like

- ➤ Locust
- ➤ Bee Bee Tree
- ➤ Crab Apple Trees
- ➤ Tulip Tree

Honeybees

Pollen can be many colors, even blue; with the most common being various shades of yellow. Pollen comes from flowers, trees, and weeds. The honeybees use pollen to eat and feed the colony.

Nectar is a nearly clear, sweet substance that is used to make honey. Honeybees find nectar in flowers.

Royal Jelly is made by the honeybees and is a super nutritious food that is fed to the queen all the time, where the other bees only get a little bit when they are maturing (growing up).

Pollination is when bees go from flower to flower spreading pollen so that flowers can make seeds then fruit.

Honeybee covered in pollen

Colony Collapse in the United States

The honeybee population is declining at an alarming rate all over the United States, and other country's too. This decline is referred to by many as Colony Collapse Disorder, or CCD, and researchers are trying to figure out reasons for their disappearance. Could this be chemically related? Perhaps the pesticides we spray on our lawns, gardens, trees, shrubs, flower beds, and field crops have caused the decline in honeybees. Researchers say pesticides are a factor that we all can control-- at least at home. No matter what is causing this collapse, to help the honeybees build back up in your area; plant a flower garden, shrubs, or trees that honeybees like from the list included in this book. Plant a wide selection of flowers with varying bloom dates to spread their blooms over spring, summer, and fall. The very best success comes from the use of plants and trees that normally grow in your area. More information about honeybees can be found by contacting a local beekeeper, the United States Department of Agriculture, or your county Extension Service.

> Honeybees are very important insects, as well as pollinators for our gardens, fruit trees, and other plants.

References & Resources

- *http://www.archive.org/details/beesandbeekeepi00harbgoog-*
  Public Domain Literature
- *Dave Wright http://www.davesbees.com – Natural Beekeeping*
- *http://www.usda.gov United States Dept. of Agriculture*
- *http://extension.osu.edu/search?SearchableText=beekeeping*

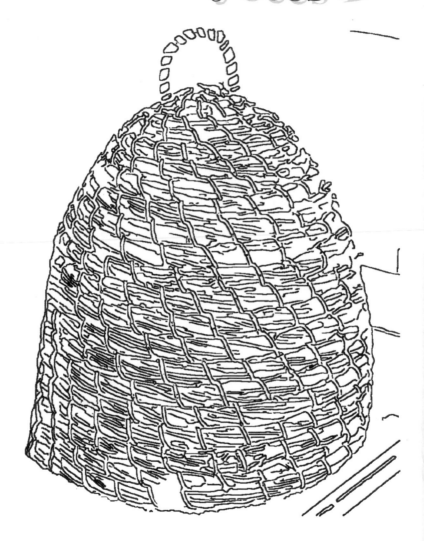

BEE SKEP

Virginia Wright

http://www.virginiawright.com

Coloring Book Pages